# DON'T BE AFRAID

A Letter to a Black Son

Shonda Rushing

Published by New Seed Industries, LLC,
West Bloomfield, Michigan
Email:  newseedllc@gmail.com
Website:  www.newseedindustries.com

Don't Be Afraid: A Letter to a Black Son
by Shonda Rushing

ISBN-13:  978-1-7369277-0-0
Printed in the United States of America

## *Thank You*

*A special posthumous thank you goes to my mother. How I wish you were here to finally see my work in print. You always believed in me and never hesitated to express how proud you always were of my accomplishments, big and small. To my eldest sister, Denise, for always doing whatever you could for me. You always believed in me. To my dearest, closest and best friend and my sister Tracey! You have always made me believe I could fly. I have often said that everyone needs someone like you. Like you, because you are taken. You have been the exact same person from day one. We have learned what friendship forged in the fire really is. I can always hear you saying, "Do it! Jump! Write it! Say it!" And the times you made me laugh hysterically when I did not want to are too many to count. To my black sons, T.J. and Brayden, for being my inspiration for everything.*

*A very special thank you goes to the original five of the Clean Your Soul Class for opening me up in ways I did not realize were possible. To Brock, for taking care of me like a big brother and always making sure I am okay.*

*And to the many of you that have prayed for me, encouraged me, believed in me, spoke life to me and checked on me often, thank you; I love you and appreciate you.*

An Uncomfortable but Necessary
Conversation

# **Contents**

# Introduction

This world can be both triggering and traumatizing for black parents. It seems like, since we first arrived in this country, there have been significant discussions that we must have with our children, especially our sons, that other ethnicities may not have to have. When our sons reach that ripe, old age of ten, we must sit them down for "the talk." I am not sure if you can imagine trying to explain to a child, whom you've told his whole life to just tell the truth, to do what you're supposed to do and everything will be okay that if you get stopped by the police, whose job it is to protect and serve, you can do everything right, obey the law, tell the truth and you can still be arrested, beaten, shot or killed. I am not sure if you understand how triggering it is when your young adult son is out past dark, the phone rings and you have a seven-second heart attack until you realize it's just your friend calling to chat with you for a bit. Because subconsciously you are always thinking it is a call to come to the police station or to the morgue to identify the body of a child who just went to the movies with his friends, the mall to buy new jeans, or made a stop at the neighborhood gas station for snacks. It is a complicated form of PTSD we have that is triggered when the phone rings because we are no longer sleeping at night until our children are safe at home. No wonder we are frustrated, irritated and angry. We are tired, and it is complicated. We are tired of the world being so loud and the church being so silent. I am a child of the '70s, not far removed from the movements of the '60s where the churches were paramount in the outcry of inequalities and injustices. We have somehow entered the "We're just gonna pray about it" movement. Don't get me wrong. There is nothing wrong with prayer, and I believe we should certainly be praying. But last time I checked, I still have black sons, and faith without works is still dead.

Ta-Nehisi Coates has said, "In America, it is traditional to destroy the black body...".[1] If you have black sons (and in some cases daughters), a black husband, nephew, dad, cousin, close friend or are black in America, this must be concerning.

And it certainly must, in some way, be woven into the fabric of the coming-of-age conversations in the household. Perhaps it won't change anything, but it is our responsibility to set our children on the best, most well-informed path possible. And even if, God forbid, the story ends in tragedy, you will have some comfort in knowing that you did the very best you could to prepare them for the duality of life they will constantly live in where you tell them they are beautiful, strong, intelligent, and powerful, but you are also seen as a threat to the majority rule,

1. Ta-Nehisi Coates, *Between the World and Me* (New York: Spiegel & Grau, 2015), 103.

are feared and hunted simply for wanting the basic rights guaranteed to all humans. I have had to explain that our ancestors were hung on trees like fruit just for wanting to be free, beaten and humiliated in the streets for trying to vote or arrested and jailed for simply wanting to sit down on the bus after a hard day's work. How many of the places they built could they not go into, and how many of the roads they paved could they not be caught walking on after dark and sometimes during the day? It's crazy, right? Yes, it is; but it is true. But it's okay, as long as you know that you are not the descendant of slaves. You are the descendant of kings and queens who were enslaved and, yet, were not broken. And neither will you be broken!

We have these tough conversations because we need your soul to be whole. That soul is the seat of your will, emotions, intentions, feelings, and decisions. Your soul is your responsibility, not God's. You must work out your own soul's salvation

(Phil. 2:12). And if your soul is damaged, so will your feelings, emotions, intentions, and decisions be. We have these talks because our children need someone they can trust with the wars of their souls so they can learn to be honest in a world that tells them to lie because the toxicity you do not heal and correct is passed on to your children. And unprocessed pain justifies bad behavior and disciples you in your own voice. We have these talks because if your soul is broken, your will, intentions, emotions, and decisions become toxic. And if you do not learn to handle that and process it, you will sabotage even your help from God, and you will replicate the surroundings of past painful experiences. But not so because I will be the cornerstone of your healing circle with authority and permission to speak into your life.

# CHAPTER I

## Open Your Eyes While You Dream: There's More

Dear Son,

I often think of the many conversations we have had about what you want to be when you grow up, and I am always immensely proud of how you are not afraid to reach. You never grab for the low-hanging fruit. I will never tell you that you cannot do that or you should try for this, but I will always equip you for the journey. I will let you know that you are one of the most beautiful creations of God's hand: a black man. And the thing that makes you so beautiful is also the thing that makes you the most feared thing in America and has been since the beginning of time. Your beautiful, black body is a commodity. When your ancestors were brought here, they were called a "beautiful piece of meat" with exceptional skills. They were long, strong, lean, and fast. They could sing, dance and make them laugh, but do not ever try to think for yourself. Because a thinking black man is a dangerous man, a weapon of massive destruction only cleansed by laying those bodies on America's altar. For the rest of your life, the world will tell you to sing, dance, run, catch, entertain me, and make me laugh because that is all they think you have to offer. They think that is all you have to offer because in your preconceived future there are two things for you: death or jail. But do not be afraid son. There is a greater plan for you and that is the ability to know the truth of who God is, who you are, and where you come from that is steeped in love, truth, and survival.

You have been taught to think for yourself and to question everything. You have never been told that you are reaching too high because your dreams are powerful tools given to you by God to lead and guide you. They shape your thoughts and give fuel to your pursuit. Never place more expectations on another than you place on yourself, and

never allow anyone to cause you to
lower what you require from yourself.
Never be afraid to be the smartest person
in the room, but never treat anyone as if
they are beneath you. Your dreams do
not require that you know all the
answers but that you always ask the
questions. When you dream with your
eyes closed, fear has a way of making
you feel as if it's always just outside of
your reach, but open your eyes so that
you can see that, that is just an illusion
and it's already inside of you. See, you
are not reaching outside to pull anything
in; you are reaching inside to pull it all
out. Open your eyes son. There is
always more for you than what you see.
Do not be afraid to want more, seek
more, and obtain more. You are not
inferior, and what you go after with your
whole heart you will have.

# CHAPTER II

## The Advantage: The Pursuit

All of this may not make complete sense to you right now, but one of the greatest advantages of being thrown into a system that is not designed for your success is that they will only give you a minuscule snapshot of your history and even that will be tainted. Why is that an advantage? I am glad you asked. It is advantageous because it sets the stage of the greatest pursuit of your life: the pursuit of "Who am I", your history, legacy, and truth. The world, or at least part of it, would have you believe you are the descendent of slaves. But no son; you are the descendent of kings, queens, princes and princesses who were captured and enslaved by savages because they saw how organized and prosperous Africa was and how strong and powerful their people were. They saw how royal they were and how they spoke to each other in their several languages. And there was great respect for hierarchy, how well built it was, how strong and powerful those men were, and how well the women took care of the children. And they came with their weapons, beat them, separated them from their family and those who spoke the same dialect, chained them like animals, packed them into the bottom of ships like sardines, and set sail across the Atlantic Ocean. Not being accustomed to this kind of treatment, introduced to these kinds of diseases of strange people, and due to the severe mistreatment, millions of them died and were tossed like pebbles into the ocean. Those who survived arrived in this barren land and this country for free, picked their cotton while maintaining the economy of which they could not be a part of, built houses they could not live in, and nursed children that did not belong to them while wondering where their own children were. They picked cotton in the sweltering heat of oppression and could not ask for a sip of water or shade. Many of your ancestors had their children while working in those cotton fields. I do not even like picking the cotton out of the pill bottle, but I want you to know that you come from loins that bend but do not break.

In your pursuit of truth, you will find that you are more powerful that you can ever imagine and more intelligent than the world will ever acknowledge. They did not have a sheet of directions, protractors, straight edges, and plumblines. They could not read the language, and they could not ask questions. They had wisdom and knowledge that had been passed from generation to generation. You come from loins that built entire cities and states, and up until not long ago, they could not even vote in those same cities. They could construct buildings with the accuracy of a skilled architect. Many of them still stand today, but they could not enter the front door of those buildings or drink from the fountains when their throats were parched. Pursue the truth Son. You come from loins that built the streets we now drive on, but just a few generations ago, your grandfather had to step off the sidewalk that was probably built by his ancestors or cross the street if there was a person who didn't look like him coming down that same sidewalk. And he didn't dare look a white man in the eye, and couldn't even think about looking at his wife or daughter if he wanted to live.

You come from great loins of men and women who created hymns of praise and worship to help bring peace and joy that is not feckless so that in the worst of times they created an atmosphere that was tolerable and conducive for healing. That is the path we still walk today: pursuing God so that we create an atmosphere that even in the worst of times is creating joy.

*Many a black boy was killed*
*For looking white women in the eye.*
*Only to discover many years later*
*That it was simply a lie.*
*But I want you to never be afraid*
*To stand tall in your truth.*
*Never let the world, one time,*
*Cause you to even pretend to be aloof.*
*Sometimes I cry about the world we*
*leave.*
*Sometimes I cry just for you.*
*But the tears of every black parent cry*
*out*
*Proof of desire is in your pursuit.*
***Pursue, overtake, and recover all son.***
***-(1 Samuel 30:8)***

# CHAPTER III

# Angry Black Man

Son, you were born in America into a system not designed for your success, creativity, beauty, or intelligence. It's designed to sit on your chest, not allow you to breathe, crush your head, not allow your intelligence to be respected, and squeeze your heart so tight that you become so desensitized to the violence around you that you do not notice it seeping into you. Even Christianity in America was not designed for you. Even in the black community, Christianity was white and meant white supremacy. Christianity and white supremacy walked hand-in-hand like those who crossed the Edmund Pettus Bridge in Selma (one day we will talk about that). How could we reconcile and receive a Christianity taught to us by white brothers and sisters confessing and professing Christianity while simultaneously imposing four centuries of slavery and segregation? But as difficult as it may be, do not let those who hunger for self-interest and power make you an angry black man and stunt your personal pursuit of God. It is a ploy to cause you to become apathetic, unable to feel and distinguish real love from manipulation, keep you soulless, unable to love correctly, and be angry. Because what happens when you do that? You pass it on to your children and create a lineage of soulless sons who are angry and abusive or passive and promiscuous daughters looking for someone to love them like their fathers never did.

I have tried to always give you room to express yourself even when you are upset, and you are allowed to be involved in decisions that affect you. Nothing about you is without you. And we have a phrase when we get upset; "We talk it out, not fight it out." I want you to know how to cope and how to handle your emotions because people who do not handle their own stuff try to work it out on other people. And what I admire so much about you is, although I have not hidden the truth from you, you

are aware of "hands up, don't shoot";
you are aware of "I can't breathe." You
see the overt and covert racism in
society and politics even if you do not
understand all the mechanics of it, and
you are still not angry and so full of
love, joy and hope. I see so much in your
inquisitive eyes, black boy, that
encourages me and causes me to still
believe. I realize that I need you just as
much as you need me. I write these
words by the light in your eyes that
illuminates my darkness.

I am not saying that you will never
get angry, because you will. You will
get so mad, at times, that it will seem as
though you can taste it. And that is
okay, but do not let it lead your
decisions, ability to respect others, or
relationships. Let that giant heart of love
you have always be the beacon and your
plumbline. Let it always be what leads
you home and be your core that balances
you. Let love be the tool by which you
measure everything.

Aside from your heart of love, that
big infectious smile that lights every

room, you never ever quit. I remember many parent-teacher conferences, and every time the question arose, "What are your strengths", your answer was always *perseverance.* And you were always right. Take that with you through every stage of life. Do not let another person's no become yours. Do not let becoming an angry black man stand in the way of being a smart black man, an intelligent black man, and a loving black man.

There is an African proverb that says, "The child not embraced by the village will burn it down to feel its warmth." I pray you never not feel embraced no matter how angry life makes you. Make time for your dreams when life is stagnate, make time for God when life is busy.

CHAPTER IV

# **Inside Man**

"'For I know the plans I have for you,'
declares the LORD, 'plans to prosper
you and not to harm you, plans to give
you hope and a future.'"

-Jeremiah 29:11[NIV].

Whether you are 5'9" or 6'3", when the world looks at you, they will see the size of your hands and feet, your black skin and tightly coiled hair and you immediately become a threat to rights, the majority rule and privilege. It won't matter that you were raised with abundant love and human decency. It won't matter that you love the skin you're in and encourage others to do the same. It won't matter that you are intelligent, well-spoken and thoughtful; it won't matter that you are well-read, enlightened and woke. It won't matter how much you love God and are created in His image. No, to the world, it will only matter what you look like, but there's a force with a voice deep inside you that roars, "There is more to you than this and more for you than that." Follow that voice.

To most women, it will only matter what you do or how much money you make. When a man talks to his friends about a potential woman, they want to know, what does she look like? When a woman talks to her girlfriends about a potential man, they want to know, what does he do? Our relating to one another and selecting potential partners to do life with has been infiltrated by this westernized thought process and has reduced us to the two most fleeting parts of us: what we look like and the job we have. But neither of these alone formulate the foundation upon which we build lasting relationships and families. Women are being conditioned to judge men's worth of being potential suitors by the length of their spine, the strength of their legs, the color of their eyes, the texture of their hair, the size of their feet and the potency of their private parts all the while ignoring whether he is fiscally responsible, can construct a complete sentence, loves God, can fix a flat, is respectful of elders or even if he will strike you in anger; but he is cute though. And men are being conditioned to exemplify that same superficiality towards women. Do not fall for that!

Other men may judge you by your sexual prowess, how many women you sleep with, how many drinks you can handle, how many rules you can break, how many fights you have been in or how many times you have been arrested. And if you do not check off all those boxes, you could be labeled as soft or, perhaps, even gay.  They will attempt to force you into crabs-in-the-barrel mentality in business by telling you that this a dog-eat-dog world and either you are the pit bull or the one wearing milk bone underwear, and instead of carving your own trail to the top, you have got to be willing to destroy another to get ahead or you are not worthy of the promotion and are weak.  But that is a lie!  You do not have to destroy another to have your own. Actually, the best way to have your own is to help another build theirs, and always remember that success is rented, never owned. Success is the map you draw for yourself because no one can tell you what it will look like for you.

Remember, your struggle is never with another man, neither is he your enemy. Your struggle and stiffest competition will always be with yourself. See, all the other voices come from outside in and there are many. As the Bible says, all are significant (1 Cor. 14:10). But there is a force with a voice from deep inside you that roars. There is more to you than this, and there is more for you than that. This inside man knows because he created you and laid every brick for your path with his own hands. He has seen all of your thoughts, heard all of your words, known of all the deeds done in your body, seen your future and said it is good. This inside man is who you truly are, void of race, ethnicity, strength, sexual prowess, whites only and coloreds only. It's just you, the creation of His hands for love and good works to the praise of God's glory. It's a representation of the vastness of beauty, diversity, strength, and power of an awesome God. Yeah, that is you who was born of God, the son of God, and an heir of God that was created to see yourself only one way: the way of your inside man.

*Who can make the darkness light?*
*Who will all your battles fight?*
*Who can make the wrong things right?*
*Who comforts you all through the night?*
*Who controls the raging seas?*
*Who has the power to guide the breeze?*
*Who causes you to fall on your knees?*
*Whom does the soul seek to please?*
*Who is He that can use me, but doesn't need me?*
*Who by the green pastures feeds me?*
*Who by the still waters leads me?*
*Who with His listening ear heeds me?*
*Who smooths the stony road we trod?*
*Who sweetens the bitter chastening rod?*
*Who ensures with peace our feet are shod?*
*Who can compare to our awesome God?*

CHAPTER V

# **Conclusion**

Son, I want to leave you with some wisdom. People believe that they have many choices in life. I believe we have only two: either you serve God or you do not, and each one comes with a cup. You do not get to see what all is in that cup until after you choose. Everything after that is only challenging you to see if you will honor the choice you have made because you are justified or condemned by what you have said. That is the multiplicity of choices that will come over your lifetime; will I honor the choice I have made or will I succumb to the pressures of guilt, shame, or fear? Choose courage over comfort every time. Be brave and vulnerable. Cry when you need to, but do not waste your tears over trivial things that are not worthy of such a gift.

Never try so hard to become who people want you to be that you forget who you are, that will only produce

more frustration, anger, and regret for
your soul to try to work out at the time
of your life that you should be enjoying
it. Read your Bible, and stand for truth.
Confront injustices in love remembering
most people you meet are broken in their
own way and are trying to recover from
their own regrets.  Hurt is inevitable, and
many times people do not realize they
are hurting you. But you think they
should know better.  This can be handled
with a small conversation. Say what you
mean and do not say it mean. The
moment you protect yourself from hurt,
you close yourself off from experiencing
the purest form of love. Pain exists
inside of love.  Consider this thought.
You know that everyone you love, you
are eventually going to lose; but you
love them anyway.

No one can break your heart, only
your expectations. So manage them and
try not to take it personally and stay
loving. Always acknowledge God, and
be thankful for everything you have.
And the things that you want, work for
them. Always be respectful, especially

when you are right, and leave the world better than you found it.

There are many things you can put on, take off, learn, and unlearn. There is a whole lot that makes up who you are, including how you absorb and process the world. But be assured that you are not relating to God one way and to people another. How you treat whom you view as the least among you is how you treat God. So be kind to those who have less than you. Learn the difference between a trauma and a trigger so that you do not go through life blaming others for the experiences you have earned for the lack of self-work. Some of your greatest pains will come from places you deemed safe because even the most sacred of places is run by humans, and they are hurting and broken too and can only reproduce after their kind. Hurting people do not produce healed people. So be patient. And never walk away from God because of people.

Dr. King once said, "In spite of the darkness of this hour, we must not despair. We must not become bitter, nor must we harbor the desire to retaliate with violence. No, we must not lose faith in our [white] brothers and sisters. Somehow we must believe that the most misguided among us can learn to respect the dignity and the worth of all human personality."[2] And many that followed him so closely, after seeing the hatred given in retribution to this nonviolence, wanted to abandon this principle and strike back with some violence of their own as is the natural human reaction. He never wavered in his commitment to love with it being the most powerful force in the universe. I wish for you to do the same. It makes you no less of a proud black man.

2.   Dr. Martin Luther King, Jr., "Eulogy for Addie Mae Collins, Cynthia Wesley, and Carol Denise McNair." Eulogy, Sixth Avenue Baptist Church, Birmingham, AL, September 18, 1963.

*Your black body is the commodity used as currency by those who seek to use and control its power.*
*But absolute power corrupts absolutely.*
*So, we fight back to claim what is ours.*
*Our ancestors' blood has flooded many fields and streets that you would never be able to clear it.*
*Our voices from your choices screams so loudly from the past that even future generations will hear it.*
*But fear not sons and daughters the sins of the past.*
*That corruption is not absolute cause you can kill the revolutionary, but not the revolution.*
*And in that we remain RESOLUTE!*

In the words of Fred Hampton, Deputy Chair of the Illinois Chapter of the Black Panther Party, **"I am a revolutionary!"**[3]

3.  Fred Hampton, n.p., n.d.

www.ingramcontent.com/pod-product-compliance
Lightning Source LLC
Chambersburg PA
CBHW060103050426
42448CB00011B/2606